D0457153

The Scottish Collection

Supernatural
SCOTLAND

HARRY CAMPBELL

HarperCollins*Publishers*

Cover image:
Crathes Castle © National Trust for Scotland, 1999

Line illustrations by David Braysher.
All other images © HarperCollins Publishers, except for those on
p. 9 © The Printer's Devil and on pp. 34, 40 © PhotoDisc, Inc. 1999

HarperCollins Publishers
PO Box, Glasgow G4 0NB

First published 1999

Reprint 10 9 8 7 6 5 4 3 2 1 0

© HarperCollins Publishers, 1999

ISBN 0 00 472325 2

Printed and bound in Great Britain by The Bath Press

Contents

Introduction

Scotland, it could be said, was a very *weird* place indeed, in the true sense of the word. The Scots' belief in the supernatural and its place in everyday life and culture persisted long after it had ceased to play a dominant role elsewhere. For example, many of the everyday trials and tribulations of life in a rural community were often put down to supernatural influences. Cattle that died suddenly were sometimes said to have been struck by 'elf-shot' (see p.38), killed by evil beings with magic arrows and harvests could be ruined by witches or angry fairies. Grown men could be lured to their deaths by various supernatural beings while even babies were at risk of being attacked by the Evil Eye, or even supplanted by a fairy 'changeling'. All sorts of precautions were necessary to prevent these calamities, many of which sought to appease malign spirits or lessen their influence.

Similarly, puzzling natural phenomena were often explained with reference to supernatural creatures. For example, a knot-hole in a piece of timber was called an 'elf-bore', while 'elf-cups' are odd-shaped pieces of stone worn into a concave shape, found for example by a waterfall. The shallow depressions sometimes found in a flat rock surface were known in some places as 'kelpies' feet', and St Elmo's fire, the static electricity that sometimes flickers around the masts of ships, was called 'red kelpies' by Scottish seamen.

Scottish mythology is known for its gruesome ideas, and the red glow in the sky caused by the Aurora Borealis or Northern Lights was sometimes seen as a pool of blood, which fell to earth in the form of red stones called 'blood stones' or 'fairy blood' (in Gaelic, *fuil siochaire*). We shall not speak of the *taghairm*, which is a kind of giant spirit-cat conjured up by spit-roasting live felines.

In what must have been a persistently harsh and often hostile natural environment, it was perhaps both inevitable and understandable that the people sought to make sense of their lives in terms of capricious and malevolent beings and powers over which they had no control. In the pages that follow we will meet the many and varied supernatural creatures found in Scottish folklore, some of the eerie powers at work and the available defences against them. Although few people would admit to believing in such things nowadays, on cold, dark and dreich nights (of which Scotland has more than its fair share), anything can seem possible…

Harry Campbell

supernatural
Beings

Fairies

The fairies of Scottish tradition bear little resemblance to the pious, prettified creatures of the sentimental Victorian imagination, with their delicate wings and innocent expressions. Scottish fairies, or *sìth*, to use the Gaelic name for them, come in various shapes and forms, and are as often as not dangerous, malicious creatures. They have what might be described as an uneasy relationship with mortals, involving some cooperation, some rivalry and much mutual suspicion. When they are not malicious, they are very often mischievous and unpredictable.

Fairies live mostly underground, in fairy 'knowes' ('know' is pronounced to rhyme with 'now'), hidden away behind little concealed doorways in the sides of hills. Their colour is green, or grey in the Northern Isles. They eat the same basic foodstuffs as humans, which indeed they often earn, borrow or steal from human sources, although in some cases they can live by somehow extracting the goodness from human food (Gaelic *toradh*, or 'foison' in archaic English) without actually eating it. Cheese with the foison removed will actually float on water.

By nature they are mysterious, unpredictable and often dangerous, although when treated with consideration they repay human kindness generously. However they can be notoriously light-fingered, 'borrowing' not only food, tools and livestock but people too.

The perils of dancing with fairies

Curiosity about our supernatural neighbours is strongly discouraged. Should you hear distant music emerging from under a hill, for example, do not be tempted to investigate. This happened once near Rosehall in Sutherland, where a man entered the fairy knowe (for such it was) and joined in the dancing. He was not seen again until a year later, but felt as if he had been dancing for only a few minutes, a common phenomenon in cases of possession by supernatural forces.

Beliefs about fairies and their supernatural powers were taken quite seriously in rural Scottish communities until relatively recent times, some of which were, after all, very remote and isolated places. Two striking examples of this are the stories of the Lewis Chessmen and the Great Auk. The Lewis Chessmen are an exceptionally fine set of 12th-century Norse chess-pieces carved from walrus ivory. Today the 84 extant pieces are variously housed in the British Museum in London and in the National Museum of Scotland in Edinburgh. They were found in 1831 near Uig on the Isle of Lewis, by a local man who was mystified by the strange box he came across among the sand dunes. When he broke it open and found the sinister little figures inside, he ran away in sheer terror, convinced that they were sleeping fairies.

The great auk is an extinct seabird, a relative of the guillemot and the razorbill, only much larger. It was flightless and not unlike a penguin in appearance. One of the last known specimens is thought to have been killed in the early nineteenth century —clubbed to death by two Hebridean islanders who though it must be a witch. After all, stumbling upon it in the dark, who wouldn't lash out against this horrible feathery monster? And of course the water-kelpie (see p.21), to name but one, was known to appear sometimes in the guise of a huge bird.

In supernatural Scotland a vast host of eerie creatures lies in wait, from the bogle to the boggart to the *glaistig* to the *gruagach* to the shoopiltie to the shellycoat, to the dreadful Nucklavee. The different types of fairies can be classified into benevolent and malevolent sorts, known respectively as the **Seelie Court** and the **Unseelie Court**. The old dialect word *seelie* means something like 'blessed' or 'innocent', and comes from the same root as the modern English word 'silly', which once meant the same. However, even the Seelie Court, while repaying favours done by mortals, was quick to revenge any insults it received and the famous brownies, often regarded as the epitome of kindness and good-naturedness, also had their dark side.

Brownies

The brownies are a well-known part of Scottish folklore, besides of course giving their name to the junior branch of the Girl Guides in Britain. What is perhaps not so well known is that brownies are found not only all over Scotland but as far south as the English Midlands, as well as having their equivalents in other mainly Celtic countries.

Unlike their namesakes in the Guides, however, brownies are male, perhaps three feet in height, with brown skins and shaggy hair, and named after the ragged brown clothes they wear. In some areas they are described as having no real noses, only small holes in their faces, and in others as having webbed hands like mittens.

Brownies are hard-working and helpful to humans – most of the time at least. They usually work alone, attaching themselves to a particular farm or household and coming out at night to do all the work left undone at the end of each day, often putting the servants to shame by their industriousness. Often a brownie will become especially attached to one particular member of the family. In some cases brownies will help out in an emergency, for

Supernatural Beings

example, by fetching a midwife. All they ask in return for their night's work is a small treat such as a bowl of milk or cream and a cake or bannock, which the house-wife would prepare specially and leave some-where in easy reach.

Apart from this, a brownie should not be offered any kind of reward, least of all clothes (much as the ragged creature might seem to be in need of them), since this would constitute a positive insult. In fact, in spite of their helpful nature, brownies are easily offended when they feel their work is being taken for granted, or being cheapened by the offer of payment. Their response to any perceived slight, even unintended, may be to with-draw their labour and leave the farm, which would be a very ill omen and can lead to financial ruin.

In extreme cases a brownie may even turn into a malicious fairy known as a *boggart*, who busies himself around the house just as industriously as the brownie, but making mischief rather than helping out. His activi-ties may range from trivial pranks like breaking or hiding things, to ruining an entire harvest.

killmoulis

There are many types of brownie, with many different names and specialised habitats. One of the more distinctive types is the killmoulis, a Lowland species inhabiting mills. Specifically, he dwells in the 'killogie' (or 'kiln-logie'), which is the little shelter at the fireplace of a kiln. Physically he is unmistakable, having a huge nose but no mouth ('mow'). Like all fairies, he is nothing if not capricious, but he helps out in various

useful ways. He can be summoned only by the miller himself, who recites the following ditty:

Auld Killmoulis, wanting the mow,
Come to me now, come to me now.
Where war ye yestreen whenI killed the sow?
Had ye come ye'd hae gotten yer belly fou.

What a coincidence that the sow is always killed just too soon for the poor killmoulis to get his belly full! Given that fairies are seditious rather than servile, crafty rather than credulous, one would think that this unconvincing appeal would have been effective for a short time only. The inescapable conclusion is that Auld Killmoulis is essentially good-natured.

Redcap

For some reason, fairies commonly wear red caps, and indeed are sometimes known as redcaps. 'Redcap' (or 'Redcap Sly') is also the name of a particular goblin, the familiar of the evil Lord Soulis of Hermitage Castle, a thirteenth-century fortress in a remote part of the Borders. Like the brownie, Redcap was a short, stocky man, but he had large fiery eyes, long straggly hair, long

sharp fangs, and claws like an eagle's at the end of his scrawny fingers. He carried a pike and wore boots made of iron, as well as the red cap that gave him his name. This cap owed its bright crimson hue to the human blood in which Redcap soaked it every so often, just to keep the colour fresh.

The only defence against this horrible creature was the Cross or the Scripture, at the sight of which he would disappear with a blood-curdling shriek, leaving one of his teeth behind him.

Usually the fairies are possessed of uncanny powers of clairvoyance, but Redcap's gifts in this area were somewhat unreliable, failing as he did to predict Lord Soulis' nasty end of being wrapped in a sheet of lead and boiled to death.

trows

In Shetland, a part of Scotland whose culture is Norse rather than Celtic, we find the trows. Fairies in Shetland wear grey, rather than green, the customary

fairy colour elsewhere, and have the peculiar habit of walking backwards when watched. The trows are related to the Scandinavian trolls and, like them, live underground. On the isle of Rhum, dense populations of Manx Shearwater live in burrows on the sides of Trollival – the 'hill of trolls' – which is so called because the Vikings believed that the unearthly cries of the seabirds were the sound of trolls.

In their underground homes the little grey people are safe from the dangerous rays of the sun, which though not fatal to trows, can trap them. If a trow is caught out above ground after dawn it cannot return home until dusk. (With the ozone hole situated directly over the north of Scotland, things must be even harder for trows than ever.)

Like many Scottish supernatural beings, trows can enter into relationships with humans, but the outcome is not usually a happy one. Some try to lure mortal women into their realm; but if they take a human wife, they can only have one child, since the wife dies as soon as their baby is born. However, a trow may benefit a family by taking it into his protection much as a brownie would. The family will prosper, unless they offend the trow, who will then turn against them and cause havoc.

Banshee

The banshee, or *bean si* (fairy woman) in Gaelic, is perhaps usually thought of as a resident of Ireland, where she is heard wailing for the dead. But in fact she exists also in the Highlands and islands of Scotland, where she is a malign visible presence. Walking by a desolate stream one may come upon a small, strange-looking woman washing clothes. She wears green, the fairy colour, and the linen she washes is in fact the blood-stained clothing of mortals who are about to die. If you should catch a glimpse of her red webbed feet, you will know for certain that this is the *bean-nighe*, the 'washing woman'.

On Islay, where she is called the *caointeach*, she is particularly dangerous, lashing out at the traveller's legs with her wet washing, which often causes paralysis. The to way to handle the sinister washer-woman is to place yourself between her and the water, which means she is forced to grant three wishes. To gain complete mastery of the situation one should attempt to grab one of her pendulous breasts and claim the status of foster-child, thereby gaining her favour.

Baobhan Sith

An equally sinister version of the banshee is the *baobhan sìth*, a sort of Celtic vampire. From Ross-shire in the far north comes the disturbing tale of the four young huntsmen, who took shelter in a remote shepherd's hut. To pass the time one of them struck up the 'mouth-music' (a kind of rhythmic wordless singing practised in Ireland and Scotland) and the others danced to his tune. All they needed now were dance-partners. Just as this thought crossed their minds, who should appear at the door but four friendly young girls, who happily joined in the merrymaking. But while the three couples capered happily, the music-maker suddenly became aware of drops of blood falling to the floor as they danced.

Panic-stricken, he fled from the hut, pursued by his new girlfriend. Finding himself suddenly less eager for her company, he wisely took cover among the four horses that stood outside. Here she could not reach him, since the horses were shod with iron, which is an excellent form of protection against evil magic. And here he was forced to remain, until the sunrise came and the *baobhan sìth* disappeared. When the young man returned to the hut he found the corpses of his four companions, from whose pallid bodies the last drop of blood had been drained.

pechs

As we have seen, some of the creatures of super-natural Scotland are memories of very ancient traditions. Among the many names of fairies, in the Lowlands, are the pechs (or pehts), and it is seriously believed that this name may reveal a folk memory of the mysterious inhabitants of Scotland known to the Romans as the Picts, literally the painted people, so-called because of their habit of painting themselves withwoad, a blue pigment. Almost nothing is known of these people, but they may have been the builders of the brochs, the intriguing round towers whose exact purpose remains a mystery. According to legend the pechs are prodigious builders, capable of erecting one of these massive structures in a single night, passing the stones

from hand to hand direct from the quarry, like Scottish pyramid-builders.

Speed was important because, like trolls, pechs cannot bear daylight and had to be securely ensconced in their new home by sunrise. Physically they are unmistakable: short and strong, about three or four feet high, with red hair, long arms and huge feet so broad that when it rains, a reasonably fit pecht, lying on his back or standing on his head, can use them as an umbrella. Thus, another characteristic they share with the trolls is that of being a gift to the souvenir industry.

fachan

One of the strangest of Scotland's fairy creatures is the fàchan, a species who could make the pechs look inconspicuous. He has only one leg, one eye in the centre of his forehead, and one hand, sticking directly out of his chest. And again, according to some, this grotesque creature may be a folk memory of the Celtic seers, who when engaged upon the process of seeing, supposedly closed one eye and took up a peculiar one-legged stance with one arm stretched forward.

Sea Monsters

Scotland is a country not only of mountains but also of waterways – and both of these are well-known as an intense focus of supernatural forces. Over most of the country, even to this day, distances are great, roads few, and the population sparse. Arms of the sea reach far inland, and even at high altitudes one finds atmospheric mountain lakelets or 'lochans'.

In total, Scotland has an amazing 16,000 km of coastline, along with innumerable bodies of water of all shapes and sizes, the deepest of which is the famous Loch Ness (some 300 metres or so) and the largest in area the equally famous Loch Lomond. The Outer Hebrides and the Northern Isles are battered by seas of oceanic ferocity, and the sea is an elemental force in daily life. The Western Highlands are almost reminiscent of Norway, with their intricate networks of lochs and sea-lochs.

Confronted constantly by such mysterious depths, often stained dark brown with peat sediments, it is easy to understand the emergence of a belief in the equally mysterious creatures that inhabit them.

Water-Kelpies

The majority of supernatural Scottish sea-creatures take the form of a horse, though they can appear in other guises too. Such animals are generically termed kelpies or water-kelpies, though they are also variously known by such evocative names as *water-trow*, *shoopiltie*, *tangie*, *noggle* and *nicker*. These creatures might reminded you somewhat of the famous inhabitant of Loch Ness, and some of the early descriptions of Nessie appear to fit well into the water-kelpie tradition, although in most accounts of her appearances, she comes across as far more shy and peaceful (and quieter!).

Like most Scottish fairy-folk, water-spirits are mischievous or even dangerous, and one is wise to beware of them. They also have a strong sense of theatre, as we shall see.

In the days when journeys were slow and tedious for those who did not have access to four-legged transport, a beautiful, friendly-looking horse standing unattended near the road would be an arresting sight for the passer-by. Often the creature would be wearing a fine harness and bridle, and the temptation to 'borrow' him for a while was great, especially to a weary traveller, late for some important errand. But once he mounted the animal, the joy-rider found himself magically glued to its back, whereupon it would tear off at great speed and plunge into the nearest running water. The victim would be lucky to escape with his life; often all that was found afterwards, floating on the surface, was his liver (or, in some versions, the heart and lungs).

However, it is sometimes possible to subdue a kelpie

and take control of his magic power. Anyone who can get close enough to put a human bridle on the fairy horse (or remove the magic bridle he wears) renders him powerless, and can use him as an ordinary beast of burden.

The most dangerous sort of water-horse is the one found in the Western Isles, known in Gaelic as *each uisge*, which lives in the sea and in lochs rather than rivers like the lowland kelpie. Not content with simply drowning its victims, *each uisge* tears them to pieces and devours them, leaving the grisly remains of its meal to float to the surface.

At other times the kelpie can be more mischievous than murderous. With their fondness for running water, kelpies can be a real nuisance to the owners of water-mills, where they like to hang onto the mill-wheel, bringing the milling process to a grinding halt. Like many fairies, they take a peverse delight in hindering human productivity, but can be placated by an offering of food. A useful precaution against kelpie trouble is to throw three handfuls of the milled grain into the hopper last thing at night, or in the case of a daytime attack, to simply scatter some meal onto the water itself.

Among other disguises, the kelpie can appear in the form of a old man. According to one story, a traveller once came upon an wizened old fellow patching his ragged trousers. As he laid out the pieces of cloth, or 'clouts', he muttered to himself "that clout'll do here, and this one'll do here..." and so on. The traveller, somehow realising (the story does not explain how) that he was looking at a kelpie and not a mortal man, leapt forward and struck him mightily on the head, with the punning cry "...and this clout'll do here!" – at which the kelpie immediately reverted to its true shape and, neighing loudly, plunged into the water. Such coolness and ready wit is unusual among the survivors of encounters with supernatural creatures.

Noggles

The noggle (also known as a neugle, nuggle, nyuggle or nygel) is a particular kind of kelpie found in the Shetland Islands. This particular water-horse is less dangerous than other varieties, but like them, it appears as a pretty horse (or a Shet-land pony in this case), conveniently equipped with saddle and bridle and fatally irresistible to passers-by. Those who get onto his back may not actually be torn to pieces as they would be in places where the fiercer sorts of water-horses are found, but they will certainly be dragged off into the water for a ducking, which will be dangerous if not fatal. Even in summer the waters of Scottish lochs and rivers run icy cold.

Here is one version of what happens when the beastie persuades someone to mount him:

> At once, with lightning speed, he makes for the nearest water – with a noise like thunder, his eyes flaming, jets of fire issuing from his mouth and nostrils, and a luminous tail like the tail of a comet stretching out behind him – and plunges in, leaving his deluded rider to his fate

As parents are forever warning their children, the waterside is a dangerous place, and sensible precautions should always be taken. As we have seen, fairy horses do bear certain tell-tale physical marks. Before attempting to misappropriate unattended horseflesh for recreational or other purposes, it is advisable to glance at the beast's ears (are they suspiciously short, or even absent?) and its tail. Whereas the tail of a normal horse hangs straight down, that of a noggle arches up in a pretty curve over its back.

In Orkney there is also a sea-dwelling kelpie, known as the tangie. It gets its name because, unlike the other water-horses with their sleek, elegant appearance, it is covered in rough hair and seaweed ('tang' in Orkney and Shetland dialect).

Nucklavee

The nastiest of the Scottish sea monsters must be Nucklavee (or Knoggelvi), a kind of Orcadian sea-centaur who emerges from the waves to rape and pillage, laying waste to crops, livestock and humans alike. According to the account of one who, long ago, had the misfortune to meet him on the road, he resembles:

> a great horse with flappers like fins about his legs, with a mouth as wide as a whale's, from whence came breath like steam from a brewing-kettle. He had but one eye, and that as red a fire. On him sat, or rather seemed to grow from his back, a huge man with no legs, and arms that reached nearly to the ground.

His head is like a man's but ten times bigger, with a wide, protruberant mouth like that of a pig. Most horrible of all, Nucklavee appears to have no skin, only raw red flesh, with

> blood, black as tar, running through yellow veins, and great white sinews, thick as horse-tethers, twisting, stretching, and contracting as the monster moved.

Some say that it is futile to try to escape from

supernatural creatures. Such people have probably never been pursued at night along the shores of a loch by a skinless monster, half human, half horse. Confronted with this creature, the nocturnal pedestrian is strongly advised to abandon all dignity and, at top speed, make for a river or stream; since like certain others of his unearthly kind, Nucklavee is incapable of pursuing his prey over running water.

Mermaids

The mermaid, the sea-creature with the body of a beautiful woman and the tail of a fish, is well-known known in many cultures. In Scotland, unlike many water-creatures, she is not afraid of fresh water and is sometimes found in rivers and lakes. For all their friendly appearance, mermaids can be dangerous. Like their deep-sea cousins, and indeed many other water-spirits, they have been known to lure inno-cent men to a watery death, for example by pretending to be drowning woman. They are also known for their skill with medicinal herbs, which is occasionally passed on to humankind. For a more typically Scottish inter-relationship between human and water-spir-it, the selkie is perhaps more representative.

Selkies

I am a man, upon the land
And I am a selkie in the sea
NURSERY RHYME

The selkie, or silkie, (also silkie, sealkie, sealchie, or selchie) is one of the best-known inhabitants of supernatural Scotland. Not all of the seals you see on the rocky shores of the are ordinary animals. Some of them, the larger ones, are selkies, which have the power to shed their seal skins on land and appear in the form of human beings. The 'selkie folk' are one of the more touching and less sinister characters in Scottish mythology.

In their human form, female selkies are known for their exceptional beauty; their huge liquid brown eyes hint at their true nature. There are many recorded cases of marriages between selkies and humans, although there is often an element of coercion and the result is never lasting happiness. For example, a mortal man might come across a group of beautiful seal-maidens playing by the shore. They take fright and rush back into the water, slipping on their discarded skins and turning back into seals. But the man has found and hidden one of the skins, thereby preventing its owner from escaping back to the sea with the others. She becomes his wife and they live together as humans for many years, though their children may bear the distinctive mark of their aquatic origins: they are born with webs between the fingers, which, if cut, cause characteristic ugly scars which leave their hands disfigured and clumsy. One day the selkie finds the skin her husband has kept hidden away for so

Supernatural Beings

long. The call of the deep is too strong for her to resist and she returns to her former life under the water, leaving him a sadder and a wiser man.

An entertaining short story by Eric Linklater tells the tale of a modern encounter with a selkie, as you may guess from the title: *Sealskin Trousers*.

Despite explanations to do with its silky pelt (hence 'silkie'), the word *selkie* – or *selchie* as it is sometimes pronounced – is simply the diminutive form of the Scottish *selch*, which is a variant of the standard English 'seal'.

The selkie is strictly speaking a creature of the northern isles (Shetland and Orkney) and Caithness. However the concept of the half-seal-half-human is widespread in Scotland. In the Western Highlands and the Western Isles, where Gaelic is the indigenous language, the name *roane* (Gaelic *ròn* = seal) is often used to refer to these fairy seal-creatures. The roane are gentle and forgiving beings, at least if the following story is anything to go by.

There was once a seal-hunter, who lived by killing seals and selling their beautiful skins. One day he caught a particularly large and handsome seal, but before he could kill it, it escaped, leaving a trail of blood. In the struggle the man's knife was lost. That night there came a knock at the door: the servant of a rich merchant bringing a large order for sealskins. "I will take you to my master to agree a price," said the man, and they both got onto his horse and raced away towards the shore. Before the hunter knew what was happening, he was being dragged underwater, down, down, down to the secret domain of the roane, where a large male seal lay badly injured. And there was the very knife that had disappeared earlier that day...

The hunter was distressed at the pain he had caused, and terrified of the punishment he might expect. But the seal-folk were not intent on revenge. They showed him how to cure the wound using a magic spell, and made him promise never to hurt another seal as long as he lived – a promise which the hunter was glad to make and which he kept until his dying day.

Worms

Scotland abounds in stories of terrifying worms, terrorizing entire districts with their murderous rages. But do not be puzzled by the incongruous B-movie vision of a gigantic mutant earthworm with the strength of many horses. 'Worm' in this case is simply a Old

English word (from Norse) meaning a kind of supernatural reptile rather like a sea-serpent or dragon. Strictly speaking, while a true dragon has the familiar attributes of wings and fiery breath, worms, supposedly Scandinavian in origin, are more like serpents, with poisonous breath.

Worms are often credited with having created the shape of the local topography. The most dramatic example of this (more in the nature of a fable than a serious belief) is the story of Mester Stoorworm, who was built on a truly epic scale. He could sweep whole towns and mountains into the sea with his tongue. He would crack castles like nutshells and suck out the inhabitants. What we now call Iceland was claimed to be the remains of the dead worm's curled-up body, while the Orkneys, the Shetlands and Faeroes were his teeth, which the monster spat out as he died.

Another famous Scottish worm is the Linton Worm, which terrorised this small community in Dumfries and Galloway until a local laird, John de Somerville, succeeded in killing it using a specially-developed spear, sheathed in iron and tipped with a burning peat dipped

in pitch, which he rammed into the beast's gaping mouth until its insides were burned out. As it thrashed about in its death-throes, the worm's coils created the spiral formations that can still be seen on – where else? – Wormington Hill.

The Big Grey Man

Ben MacDhui is a peak in the famous Cairngorm range, in fact the second highest mountain in Scotland at 4296 feet (1309 metres). And if the brochs are Scotland's pyramids, the Big Grey Man is Scotland's yeti. Unlike many of the other creatures decribed here, he is a fairly recently phenomenon, first encountered in 1891, in the form of a giant shadowy figure given to pursuing climbers off the mountain. Physical descriptions are generally vague: tall and hairy, and above all deeply sinister, filling climbers with a nameless terror and even a disregard for their own safety in their headlong rush to escape. More specifically, and rather more bizarrely, according to one report, he wears a top hat.

the Devil

The Devil is an important figure in Scotland, as a wealth of proverbs, placenames and nicknames go to show.

Among the many picturesque placenames of Scotland the Devil finds his Elbow, his Staircase, two Cauldrons and even a Beeftub. He is known variously as the Earl of Hell, the Big Brindled One, the Auld [old] Man, the Bad Man, the Black [swarthy] Man, the Auld Chiel [lad], Auld Hornie, Auld Clootie or Cloots (a reference to cloven hoofs), and in Gaelic *Muc Mhor Dhubh* [The Big Black Pig]. The last of these points to a strange and little-known Scottish cultural phenomenon: the High-land taboo on pork-eating. Strangely perhaps, in a country where wild boar survived until the late 17th century, pigs were not often kept or eaten in the Highlands, and indeed were somehow associated with the Evil One.

In Scotland, until much later than elsewhere, the Devil was felt to be very a much a real person, often with a real physical presence. By the time of Robert Burns (the late 18th century), in whose work he has a prominent role, we see him portrayed slightly satirically. Yet within recent memory he had been no laughing matter. The previous century is full of accounts of his appearances in person. His physical appearance is variable, in that he can assume the form of any animal he likes, usually black or 'tanny' (brindled). Appearing in his own shape he is the well-known swarthy figure, sometimes with cloven hooves and the horns that reveal his connections with the Celtic horned gods of the ancient world.

Donald Mackay, the 17th-century Lord Reay, is famous for his dealings with the Bad Man. Nicknamed the Wizard of Reay, he was known to have studied the evil arts under the Man himself, in Italy. At the end of the last lesson of term most pupils are keen enough to get away, but at this school there was an extra incentive to make a smart exit, since the teacher's habit was to grab the last to leave and claim him as his disciple. As the Earl of Hell lunged for the Chief of the Clan Mackay, the latter shouted out "De'il tak the hindmost!" and left his adversary holding only his shadow, which was in fact the very last thing out of the door. Thereafter, he never cast a shadow, even on those rare occasions when the sun shines brightly in the Highlands.

Nor was this Donald's only near escape from the Devil. In a sea-loch near the small town of Durness in Sutherland, Smoo Cave forms a suitably atmospheric setting for this tale. When his

Smoo Cave

dog came howling out of the limestone caverns with not a hair left upon his back, Earl Donald knew that his old adversary had returned to claim his dues. Luckily, just at that moment a cock crowed, a sound which with its connotations of daylight is a natural antidote to supernatural forces. The Devil and the squad of witches with him flew off in a rage, blasting holes through the rock that can still be seen today.

Any odd marks or unexplained physical curiosities tended to be linked with Auld Clootie, such as the strange parallel grooves in the stone of the Kirk of Lady on Sanday in Orkney. These look as if someone had been dragged away, hanging on by their fingernails, and are known as the Devil's Fingermarks.

As we have seen, the Devil can assume many disguises, even that of a man of God. At Auchtermuchty in Fife the villagers had such a reputation for piety that he was forced to take on the shape of a minister. His preaching was so compelling that the trick nearly succeeded, but just in time one of the congregation spotted the cloven hoofs under the cassock. Foiled, the Auld Chiel took off at high speed across the sky.

The Big Brindled One is very much a gambling man, and fond of a game of chess too. In a secret

The Devils's Bones

room somewhere in Glamis Castle, the evil Earl Beardie, infamous for gambling on the Sabbath, sits to this day playing dice with the Devil, even though he died five centuries ago. Not for nothing are dice known as the Devil's Bones (or Teeth).

Alexander Stewart, the 14th-century Earl of Buchan, known as the Wolf of Badenoch for his brutal pillaging of the Highlands, also dabbled in witchcraft. On night he was observed in Ruthven Castle playing chess with a mysterious horseman dressed in black. "Check!" cried the stranger, at which a ball of fire swallowed them up. The next day the burned remains of the Wolf and his men were found in the castle; but he and the Black Man are still sometimes seen playing chess together.

Just as he often does in the Bible, the Devil is known for taking possession of humans. This surely helps to explain the Calvinist suspicion of lively music and dancing, involving the risk of loss of self-control; the 'bewitching' ability of a good tune to change one's mood and make one lose all sense of time. Sure enough, the Earl of Hell often appears as a musician, especially a fiddler or piper.

The fairies often performed the same tricks, but whereas they are often linked with an older, pre-

Christian traditions, the Devil as we know him in recent centuries represents an element of formalised religion. However much folklore may be involved in such beliefs, they were justified through reference to the Bible, as was his role in the cult of witchcraft that raged so strongly in Scotland in the seventeenth century. 'The De'il's aye guid to his ain [always good to his own]' they said; and his own were those who he had been recruited to his supernatural world: witches (see p.47)

supernatural powers

elf-Shot

The supernatural powers are many, and cause plenty of trouble to humans, although remedies and talismans do exist. For example, if your fields or beasts are not yielding as they should, the fairies may be behind it. (In this respect their powers overlap with those of witches, when the blame adheres to a real person such as an unpopular neighbour, with horrifying consequences in the case of the notorious witch-hunts of the 17th century.) It sometimes happens that healthy animals simply drop dead in the field. Such sudden deaths may seem inexplicable, but in fact they are caused by 'elf-shot'. The beast has in fact been picked off by malicious fairies or agents of the Devil using magic arrows. The proof of this is freely visible in the form of those flint arrowheads that often turn up in the fields – these are actually spent fairy ammunition.

The evil eye

The Evil Eye (Gaelic: *an droch-sùil*) is a belief found throughout Europe, surviving today all around the Mediterranean, where bad luck is kept away by little pieces of blue glass, and fishing boats are kept safe by an eye painted on the bows. In Scotland as elsewhere it can be dangerous to praise a baby too highly, in case the fairies hear and are jealous. Rather than say "what a beautiful child!", one should comment on how ugly it is, to reduce the risk of its being stolen away or replaced with a changeling.

Changelings

If your newborn child seems somehow 'not quite right', is excessively demanding or slow to thrive, or generally fails to give satisfaction in any way, it may be because it is not actually the same child you gave birth to. It may have been stolen by the fairies and replaced with a 'changeling'. This supernatural substitute might be one of several things: a worn-out geriatric fairy, of no further use to her own sort, who wants the chance of an easy life; or a fairy weakling, a young one who is a burden and needs extra attention; or even just a carefully carved piece of wood, magically given the lifelike appearance of the human baby, who is stolen away to add vigour to the fairy gene-pool. Fairies often seem to need human help in matters of childcare.

When the presence of a changeling is detected, there are various methods of trying to force the fairies to take back this cuckoo in the nest, many of which involve treating the child with extreme cruelty, such as for example throwing it on the fire, so that it flies away back to its own kind. Sadly, such beliefs caused horrific brutalities to be committed on infants who presented some unexplained peculiarity.

A kinder technique involves trying to make the fairy

impostor laugh, by some incongruous act such as boiling water in eggshells. "I'm fifteen hundred years in this world," cried one changeling thus surprised, "and I never saw that before."

Glamour

Of course fairies are usually invisible, which is because of 'glamour', a kind of visual magic. (The modern sense of this word, meaning allure or prestige, grew from an earlier kind of 'charm' – the magic sort.) This enchantment acts on human eyes to control what they can see. It can be broken by a special fairy ointment, or a simple four-leafed clover. For example, fairies are well-known for taking their share of the milk from cows, but are rarely caught in the act. Once, a milkmaid happened to pick a four-leafed clover in the handful of grass she used as a pad to cushion weight of the milk-pail she carried on her head. Suddenly she could see teams of tiny fairies carefully extracting the last drops from the cow she had just milked.

Another way fairies call on human resources is by borrowing midwives to help at fairy births. When a human midwife is called to a fairy confinement she will usually see only a human house, albeit one she had never

40

seen or visited before. She is given a special ointment to rub onto the eyes of the newborn fairy; but if she should happen to touch her own eyes with it as well she will see the place for what it really is. In some cases she is given the use of the ointment for the duration of the birth.

Taboos

To avoid the danger of fairy intervention, many taboos have grown up in Scottish lore. On of the peculiarities of the fairies is their touchiness, and so it is wise to refer to them by flattering names: the Good People (in Gaelic, *Sleagh Maith*), the Fair Tribe, the Little Folk, the Grey Neighbours and so on.

Names in fact have powerful magical qualities. For this reason, it is advisable to baptise children as soon as possible, since in the nameless state they are particularly vulnerable to being stolen away and replaced with a changeling. In the north-east, the sad unquiet spirits of babies who have died unbaptised are known as 'tarans'.

Conversely, one can gain power over an adversary by knowing his name, as we see from the tale of Whuppitie Stoorie. ('Stoor' is Scots for 'dust', a reference to those mysterious swirls of dust one sometimes sees, which are actually caused by fairies). In Orkney a similar tale is told of Peeriefool (little fool), while elsewhere he is turns up as as Rumpelstiltskin and Tom Tit Tot. In each of these tales,, a fairy performs a favour for a mortal woman in dire straits, and extracts a high price, such as her only child. It is a bargain she can only be released from if she can discover the fairy's secret name. In the end she does and the fairy never troubles her again.

A more curious taboo prohibits idly swinging the pot-hook that hangs above the fireplace. This is because a sort of brownie known as Wag at the Wa' [wall] loved nothing better than to swing back on forth on it, and to set it swinging was to invite him to appear. Now that cooking on an open fire is a thing of the past, his visitations are rarely a problem.

Charms

Luckily, there are various forms of protection against fairy forces. The obvious Christian symbols of the Cross, the Bible and holy water are protective against all sorts of supernatural forces. Other more ancient talismans such as salt, bread, fire and iron (ideally in the form of a cross) are widely effective too, as are bells of any sort. The crowing of a cock has broken many an evil spell. Rowan (the tree, its wood or its berries) is a powerful defence against magic, as is of course the well-known horseshoe. As we've seen, the four-leafed clover (now loosely associated with good luck) is also known for breaking through fairy glamour and granting

A rowan cross, a powerful protection against dark supernatural forces

the ability to see those things normally only visible to them. Less well-known is the technique of suspending a pair of scissors (providing both iron and the cross) over the crib of an unchristened child.

Strangely-shaped stones have great mystical significance; for example, self-bored stones (ones with a hole bored through them by the action of water) are very useful for protecting horses against fairy theft. You hang them like beads on a string just above an animal's stall, so that any fairy attempting to ride off on it will be swept off its back. Looking through the hole in such a stone may grant the power of second sight or the ability to see fairies.

The Fairy Flag

Dunvegan Castle, the ancestral home of the MacLeods of Skye, contains their most precious heirloom, an intriguing relic known as the Fairy Flag (*bratach sìth* in Gaelic). It is a large, tattered silk banner, of unknown age and provenance.

Examination of the fabric hints at an eastern origin, such as Syria or Rhodes and it may originally have been a shirt. Among several accounts of its origin, it is sometimes said to have been brought back from the Crusades, a gift or trophy from some supernatural source. Some link it to a flag brought to Britain in 1066 by the Norse king Harald while another story says it was left by the fairy wife of the clan chief, to keep their child warm.

Whatever its origins, the Flag is a powerful talisman

Dunvegan Castle, home of the Fairy Flag

as well as a trophy. When unfurled it is said to make the bearer invincible - although the spell only works three times, and has already been invoked twice, in 1490 and 1520. During the Second World War, photographs of it were carried into battle by members of the clan. Perhaps its main function today is magically drawing tourists to Dunvegan Castle.

Second Sight

Second sight (in Gaelic, *an dà sealladh*, the two sights) is the mystical ability to see the future, especially in terms of foretelling a death or a future wife. It is a power granted by certain methods, and to certain mortals. For example the seventh son of a seventh son, as well as having the power of curing skin diseases by touch, was often a seer (in Gaelic *taibhsear*). Now that the average size of families is diminishing, those achieving the gift by this method must be rare indeed.

Today a crystal ball or the leaves left in a teacup may be the key to the future. In the past, however, the Romans would examine the entrails of a chicken for omens, and the Scots too sometimes used an animal carcass. The Gaelic for divination is *slinneanachd*, literally the art of telling the future by examining the shoulder-joint (*slinnean*) of a sheep. Though it sounds messy, it is perhaps a more pleasant method than spending the night wrapped in a cowhide which was an alternative method of divination.

The Brahan Seer

As we have noted, looking through a self-bored stone sometimes allows one to see remarkable things and thus it was with the Brahan Seer, a kind of Scottish Nostradamus. His name was Kenneth McKenzie, or in Gaelic *Coinneach Odhar* (literally, Dun-coloured Kenneth) and he was a native of Lewis in the Outer Hebrides, at least according to a nineteenth-century account of his prophecies. But as befits an exponent of the mysterious arts, little is known for certain of the man, even down to his name. Certainly there was a Keanoch Ower indicted for witchcraft in 1577, but the source of his nickname, Brahan Castle on the Cromarty Firth, did not actually exist in his lifetime.

His activities as a clairvoyant began in the nick of time, when, looking through a self-bored stone given him by the fairies, he saw that his food that day had been poisoned by his cousin's wife. After this promising start, he went on to issue prophecies on a multitude of subjects, from the Battle of Culloden in 1746 to the coming of the railways a hundred or so years later.

At the end of his life Kenneth had the status of official Seer to the Mackenzies of Seaforth. When the clan Chief went to Paris on government business, during the rein of Charles the Second, the Countess of Seaforth asked Kenneth what was taking him so long. This put him in a delicate position; in attempt to be diplomatic he replied "Your Lord is now in a grand room, far too agreeably occupied to think of leaving Paris yet." Occupied with his mistress, of course. The truth was eventually wormed out of the Seer and he was put to death by the furious wife of his master, burned in a barrel of tar as was the fate of witches. His final prophecy was a detailed prediction of the downfall of the house of Seaforth which, according to his supporters, later came true. However, the story of the Seer's death is completely discounted by historians.

thomas the Rhymer

The name of Thomas of 'Ercildoune' (now Earlston) first occurs in a 1260s charter. His prophetic writings caused him to be known as True Thomas. He is thought to be the father of vernacular Scottish poetry, credited in one copy as the author of the 13th-century *Romance of Sir Tristem*.

The story about him is that he spent seven years in Fairyland, and was recalled there at the end of his life by the Fairy Queen. His prophecies, like those of the Brahan Seer, are taken to refer to events continuing into the twentieth century, from the crowning of Robert the Bruce, to the Battle of Flodden (1513), to the return of Field Marshall Earl Haig to his ancestral family estates in 1921.

A woodcarving depicting Thomas riding off the Fairyland with the Queen of the fairies

Witchcraft

Scotland is famous, or perhaps infamous, for its witches. Of course in a pre-scientific age, every old wife would have her stock of pet cures, herbal remedies and so on, which frequently crossed the blurred line into the mystical or supernatural. Such 'wise women' must have been part of daily life since time immemorial. In the Middle Ages, however, witchcraft began to be associated more directly with evil powers and specifically with the Devil. Witches were well-known for (like the fairies) stealing milk, spoiling harvests, raising storms, sinking ships, depriving food of its goodness, and generally inflicting suffering on their enemies.

Although the heyday of the witchcraft trials was the mid 17th century, beliefs about witches long predated this — and lingered on too, to the extent that as late as 1878 a young man in Dingwall attacked an old woman he claimed had cast a spell on his fishing-boat. He was attempting to draw blood and thus break the spell, and when tried for assault, objected that "the Bible orders us to punish witches".

Charms

Ticking pins into a model of one's enemy is perhaps something we associate today with voodoo. But the clay effigy, or *corp créadha*, as it is known in Gaelic, is also part of the stock-in-trade of Scottish witches. Sometimes pins were stuck in it; sometimes it was roasted in front of a fire as a torture; and perhaps most sinisterly of all, it was sometimes left in a stream to melt quietly away in the running water, while the victim dwindled inexorably, faded and died.

Various counter-measures were available. On the isle of Tiree, for protection against milk theft, they would leave a ball of hair in the milk, a charm that had to be renewed at Lammastide every year. A more curious defence against the evil arts is the witch-bottle. Filled with the victim's urine, and sometimes iron nails and an animal heart, it would be corked up and heated on the fire; sooner or later the witch, afflicted with a corresponding sensation of burning and blockage, would be forced to reveal herself and beg for relief.

The rise of the witch-hunts may ironically have to do with the decline of belief in, or at least official acceptance of, the religious rituals mentioned earlier on as defences against supernatural forces. When such things as candles, bells and holy water were dismissed by the Reformation as Papist superstition, people felt more vulnerable to the works of the Devil, who was still very much believed in and just as active as ever. Even the virtuous were not considered invulnerable, in a physical sense, to the menace of witchcraft. People turned instead to bizarre remedies like the witch bottle; and succumbed to the vicious paranoia of the time.

Witch-hunts

Thus when the cows ran dry or the milk would not turn to butter or the boats failed to catch any fish, suspicion might fall on any unpopular or odd character in the area. Such accusations began to be taken very seriously by religious and civil authorities, and although the hysterical witch-hunts of the early 17th century were by no means confined to Scotland, they were particularly rabid there, and interrogations especially brutal. Between 1563 (when witchcraft was made illegal) and 1736 (when the laws were repealed), several thousand people were put to death as witches in Scotland. As the Bible says, "Thou shalt not suffer a witch to live" (Exodus 22:18) and the

Scots were fervant aherants of the Good Book.

An allegation of witchcraft might stem from something quite trivial, such as someone's strange appearance or a petty dispute between neighbours, before escalating into a familiar pattern of accusation, torture, wild 'confessions', incrimination of others and barbaric execution. Such allegations would be assiduously followed up by the authorities.

First they would send in a 'pricker', a sort of freelance witch-hunter equipped with a long, sharp bodkin. He would examine the body of the alleged witch for any odd blemishes on the skin, such as scars or moles. This was the 'devil's mark', left by his claw in the process of baptising the witch into his service. The accused would be blind-folded and the needle driven into the skin: if no pain was felt it meant that she was indeed a witch. Since witch-prickers were often paid a sum for each witch found, the result was almost always positive, and they are suspected of having used tricks like retracting needles and local anaesthetics.

After this, the accused was in an almost unwinnable situation. If she refused to confess

A witch-hunter's pricker

immediately she would be tortured, in order to obtain not only a confession but the names of other witches and details of their activities. Sleep deprivation was a first step, but in Scotland more brutal methods were in common use. Standard techniques involved the 'boots' (a device for gradually crushing the bones of the legs with wedges), pilnie-winks (thumbscrews) and being 'thrawed' with a rope tightened around the head. Confessions thus extracted, often scripted by the interrogators according to standard formulas, were sometimes withdrawn later, but by then it was too late: the witch would not be 'suffered to live'. The classic form of execution was by being burned in a tar barrel. Usually the victim was strangled first, though burning alive was also possible.

Particularly notorious witch-trials took place in Auldearn (1662), North Berwick (1591), Paisley (1697) and Pittenweem (1705), brief accounts of which are given in the Gazetteer.

Not all witches were female. One of the most famous Scottish warlocks is Michael Scott (?1160-?1235), who was mentioned by Dante and Walter Scott, among others. He was essentially a scholar, famous for his knowledge of Arabic and astronomy, but became known as a wizard who learned his craft in Italy and taught witches to plait sand (you can sometimes see such natural 'ropes' on Scottish beaches). According to tradition he was the tutor of Lord Soulis of Hermitage Castle, another well-known sorcerer (see p.13). Other famous names are Sir Robert Gordon of Gordonstoun; Alexander Skene (1680-1274), who is sometimes the hero of the tale of graduation from the Devil's school, told above of Donald Mackay (see p.32); and a certain

Major Weir, who was actually tried as a witch in Edinburgh in 1670. A pillar of the Presbyterian church, formerly commander of the city's garrison, he voluntarily confessed at the age of 69 to a long list of unspeakable acts committed with his sister, Grizel. He and she were both burned, along with the staff the major always carried, and which he now claimed had a life of its own. The possibility of mental illness was dismissed by the investigators of the time, but today seems inescapable.

By the end of the 17th century the hysteria had largely abated, but superstitions lingered on and occasionally reared their heads again. The last Scottish witchcraft trial took place in 1727, at Dornoch in Sutherland. Janet Horne was accused of 'hag-riding' her daughter, who had some kind of deformity of the hands and feet which it was decided must be caused by the shoes fitted to her by the Devil. After her mother was burned as a witch, the daughter gave birth to a child with the very same genetic peculiarity. In another, gentler, time her deformity would perhaps have been explained in terms of the tales about the offspring of humans and selkies (see p.27).

Gazetteer of Supernatural Sites

As we have seen, Scotland is alive with supernatural beasts, forces, and powers. Here, for the curious – and the cautious – are some of the key sites of supernatural Scotland, along with a brief summary of their claim to fame.

Arbroath (Angus)

It is said that no communion was ever held at the 11th-century church of St Vigeans between 1699 and 1736. The church is supposed to be constructed on a base of iron bars ferried by water-kelpies (see p.21), under which lies a subterranean lake. When the minister committed suicide, fulfilling the first part of a local prophecy, it was decided that to celebrate communion there would be too dangerous in the light of the second half of the legend: that one day the church would sink into the ground. Finally a determined incumbent held the service, while the village held its breath. Disappointingly, the church remained rock-steady.

Ardblair Castle, Blairgowrie (Perthshire and Kinross)

Haunted by the mysterious Green Lady (Jean Drummond), an ill-starred lover who fell for one the Blairs, her family's bitter enemies.

Ashintully (Nr Kirkmichael, Perthshire and Kinross)

Another Green Jean (Spalding) haunts the castle where she and her maid were murdered by a jealous uncle.

Auldearn (Highland District)

Perhaps the most famous of all Scottish witches, Isabel Gowdie, was tried here in 1662. She confessed to a long catalogue of crimes, beginning when she had been baptised in her own blood by the Devil from the pulpit of the church. The activities of her 13-strong coven had included the usual interference with harvests and milk-cows, raising storms, torturing effigies and so on; and she had also copulated with the Devil and flown around magically on a piece of straw. The strangest thing about this confession, concerning events that had taken place fifteen years before, is that it was freely offered, without torture, for reasons which remain unclear.

Auldgirth (Dumfries and Galloway)

The Devil called by here in search of a wife. The husband watched with resignation as his spouse was carried off, and a few days later she returned, having been expelled from Hell for her excessive use of foul language.

Brodesbeck (Dumfries and Galloway)

The brownie inhabiting Brodesbeck Farm, near Moffat, was a particularly industrious one, but also particularly quick to take offence. One harvest-time the farmer tried to show his appreciation by leaving a little food out for him – but the only result of this well-meaning gesture was the immediate departure of the brownie, along with all the farm's good luck.

Claypots (Dundee)

This castle, near Broughty Ferry on the north bank of the Firth of Tay, was the home of a brownie so house-proud that he was driven to despair at the low standards of the paid staff and eventually left the household.

Cononbridge (Highland Region)

The River Conon is known for its magic otters. On catching one the hunter had to choose either to let the beast go in return for a wish, or kill it for valuable trophies such as the skin, which gave the wearer protection from both steel points and bullets, and the liver, which had an even more remarkable use. Licking it conferred the useful power of healing burns with one's tongue.

Corgarff (Aberdeenshire)

A man hurrying to his wife's sickbed had a close encounter with a water-kelpie – and escaped. The bridge over the river Don having been swept away, he incautiously accepted a ride with what turned out to be a kelpie, but managed to swim to safety. The frustrated creature flung a boulder after him, known to this day as 'the kelpie's stone'.

Cortacht Castle (Angus)

Haunted by the ghost of a drummer who was put to death by being thrown from the tower (or, some say, burned alive). As is usual with ghostly musicians, he is heard again whenever death is coming to the family.

Crathes Castle (Aberdeenshire)

Haunted by the ghost of a young girl who fell pregnant by one of the servants of the laird whose protection she

Gazeteer

was under. She is sometimes seen carrying the child around, and is known, conventionally enough, as the Green Lady.

Delnabo (Fife)

Scene of domestic strife between a pair of goblins, who kept the whole neighbourhood awake with their violent squabbling. In the end the male was shot dead by a farmer, and its wife had to be driven off with a bowl of scalding water.

Dunstaffnage Castle (Nr Oban, Argyll and Bute)

As very often in the more historic Scottish castles, momentous events in the life of the incumbent family are heralded by ghostly apparitions. The name of the ghost is, naturally, the Green Lady.

Duntrune Castle (Argyll and Bute)

A bagpiper was once sent by his master to infiltrate this castle, near Lochgilphead. He posed as a wandering minstrel in order to investigate the fortifications, which were formidable, but eventually his cover was blown and he was taken prisoner. As his master's army approached, he tried to warn them to stay away by piping at them. He succeeded, and had his hands cut off as a punishment; but his ghost plays very well without them.

Ednam (Borders)

Site of a fairy knowe (or Pictish burial mound) where a piper in search of fairy tunes entered – but did not return.

Fordell (Fife)

When the miller of Fordell poisoned some of·

Cromwell's soldiers who had molested his wife, their comrades had their revenge by stringing up his apprentice, and the ghostly body is still seen swinging there.

Forres (Moray)

Haunt of the three witches of Shakespeare's play Macbeth. In real life witches were burned here, after being rolled down Cluny Hill in barrels. A mysterious sickness afflicting the 10th-century King Duff (Dubh) was supposed to have been caused by witches found here torturing a wax effigy of him.

Fyvie Castle (Aberdeenshire)

The wife of Alexander Seton died in 1601, and she turned out to be a jealous ghost. When Seton remarried soon after, his wedding night was disturbed by the sound of heavy sighing; and the next day the ghost was found to have written her name outside the window of the bridal chamber. In life she was Dame Lilias Drummond; but her ghost is known as – what else? – the Green Lady.

Gight Castle (Nr Methlick, Aberdeenshire)

A piper once set out to explore an underground passage from the castle, but never returned; and his ghostly music is still heard from time to time.

Glamis Castle (Angus)

There are many hundreds of castles in Scotland but Glamis is one of the most famous. It has strong royal associations, being the ancestral home of the Bowes-Lyon family, where the Queen Mother was brought up and Princess Margaret was born; but it is also rich in ghosts, witches and diabolical associations. This has claims to be the most haunted castle in Scotland: a Grey Lady haunts the chapel, a mad earl walks the ramparts, a black page-boy is sometimes seen waiting patiently outside the Royal Apartments, and a lady roams the park with her tongue torn out. Meanwhile in a secret room, perhaps tucked away in the 4-metre-thick walls, the wicked Earl Beardie is locked up for all time with the Devil, playing dice – his punishment for gambling on the Sabbath. The unfortunate Lady Glamis, accused of poisoning her husband, was burned as a witch in 1537.

Glencoe (Highland Region)
The historical site of this famous massacre has attracted its fair share of legends, such as bands of fairy pipers leading the Campbell troops into the snow, away from their victims. Sadly, such diversionary techniques were of little help to the thirty-eight murdered MacDonalds.

Glenelg (Highland Region)
A crofter called John McInnes was drowned by a water-kelpie in the late 19th century, in the loch that now bears his name.

Glen Esk (Angus)
Haunt of another ghost piper – not murdered or executed, but stolen away by the fairies. But they failed to silence his music.

Glen Etive (Argyll and Bute)
Home of the Glen Etive fàchan (see p.19).

Glenmore Forest (Highland Region)
Home of *Lamh Dhearg* (Red Hand), a ghostly giant bearing a bloody broadsword and much given to challenging passers-by to a fight to the death.

Inverness (Highland Region)
Burial-place of Thomas the Rhymer (p.46). A phantom army is sometimes seen in full combat on the moors near Loch Ashie.

Langton House, Gavinton (Borders)
The Coburn family had a lucky escape one night when fairies tried to repay a grudge by carrying off the entire house. As the fairy demolition squad were working away

at the foundations, someone woke up and scared them off.

Largo Law (Fife)

This volcanic formation is actually a piece of rock dropped by the Devil as he rode past. The cloven-footed one has had a not inconsiderable influence on the topography of Scotland.

Loch Fyne (Argyll and Bute)

Loch Fyne is the site of an unusual apparition: an amphibious ghost ship, sailing up the loch and continuing overland.

Muchalls Castle (Nr Stonehaven, Aberdeenshire)

Rushing to meet her lover's boat, a young woman slipped and drowned. To this day she is seen brushing her hair in the mirror, getting ready to meet him. You will not be surprised to learn that her name is the Green Lady.

Noltland Castle (Orkney)

Noltland Castle, on the remote Orcadian island of

Westray, features both an energetic brownie and a ghost dog, whose howling heralds a death in the family. Meanwhile a spectral light shines to announce a birth or a marriage.

North Ballachulish (Highland Region)

A curiously-shaped stone on the banks of Loch Leven is testimony to an encounter between Sir Ewen Cameron of Lochiel and Gormul, a *cailleach* or hag. He wisely hurried towards the ferry, knowing she would be unable to follow him across the river, but she called out "my blessings on you, Ewen". He skilfully deflected this dangerous benediction with the cry "your blessings on yonder grey stone!". The laird was unharmed; but the stone was rent asunder, and so it remains to this day.

North Berwick (East Lothian)

Site of witchcraft trials in 1591, surrounding an alleged attempt to sink the king's ship by various methods including drowning a cat in the sea.

Paisley (Renfrewshire)

The Christian Shaw witch-hunt of 1697 shows remarkable similarities with the famous 1692 trials in Salem, Massachusetts. This 11-year-old girl claimed to be tormented by witches, and began vomiting up pins, eggshells, stones and other foreign bodies. Seven of those she accused were executed. Much later the evidence of her fraud was uncovered, but Shaw emerged quite unscathed from the whole affair.

Pittenweem (Fife)

Scene of one of the most notorious witch-hunts . Janet

Cornfoot, incriminated under torture by Beatrix Lang, was seized by the mob, stoned and crushed to death under a door, with the connivance of the authorities.

Ruthven Castle (Highland Region)

Here the Devil played chess with Alexander, the 'Wolf of Badenoch' (see p.35).

Schiehallion (Perthshire and Kinross)

The name of this mountain means, in Gaelic, "the fairy hill of the Caledonians". Travellers passing this spot have often described being followed by a mysterious black dog-shadow. Also strong in supernatural associations is Rannoch Moor, the bleak expanse of marsh (once forest) at its foot, sometimes said to be the largest uninhabited wilderness in Britain.

Stirling Castle (Stirling)

Stirling Castle, one of the most impressive and most visited in Scotland, naturally has a Green Lady. In fact, it has at least two ghosts, of different colours. The other is the Pink Lady.

Trotternish, Isle of Skye (Highland Region)

Home of the ghost known as *Colann gun Cheann* (The Headless Body), whose unusual method of dispatching his victims was to throw his own head at them. One day a certain young man with particularly quick reactions caught the head on the point of his sword, thereby depriving his assailant of ammunition and extracting a promise to leave the area alone in future.

Strathpeffer (Highland Region)

The Devil does his laundry here, as you can tell from the

black colour produced by the mingling of waters from sulphurous and iron-bearing springs.

Tynron (Dumfries and Galloway)
Haunted by a headless ghost, decapitated when he was chased over a cliff by the brothers of the girl he was courting.

Vallay (off North Uist, Western Isles)
This small island off North Uist was the site of a particularly barbaric witch execution. She was buried up to her neck in the gateway of a cattle-fold, so that the beasts trampled her to death. The pit is still visible to this day.

West Wemyss (Fife)
Yet another ghost of the name of 'Green Jean' haunts Wemyss castle. If the name seems at all unoriginal to you by now, it should perhaps be remembered that green, the 'fairy colour', has strong supernatural associations; and that 'Jean' rhymes with 'green'.

Gazeteer

COLLINS

Other titles in *The Scottish Collection* series are:

ISBN 0 00 472326 0

ISBN 0 00 472259 0

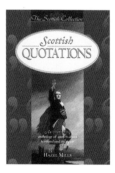

ISBN 0 00 472304 X

Classic Malts   Scottish Recipes   Scottish Verse

Homelands of the Clans